LET'S PLAY FLUTE!

FOR BEGINNERS OF ALL AGES

by Elisabeth Weinzierl & Edmund Waechter

To access companion recorded accompaniments online, visit:
www.halleonard.com/mylibrary

Enter Code
3166-3518-9784-1958

If you require a physical CD of the online audio that accompanies this book, please contact Hal Leonard Corporation at info@halleonard.com.

Sy. 2825

RICORDI

HAL•LEONARD® CORPORATION
7777 W. BLUEMOUND RD. P.O. BOX 13819 MILWAUKEE, WI 53213

Original publication: *Flöte Spielen Band A*, by Elisabeth Weinzierl and Edmund Waechter (Sy. 2675)
© 2001 by G. Ricordi & Co.
All rights reserved

English translation/adaptation: *Let's Play Flute! Method Book 1*, by Elisabeth Weinzierl and Edmund Waechter
English translation/adaptation by Richard Laughlin and Rachel Kelly, edited by Rachel Kelly
© 2015 by G. Ricordi & Co.
All rights reserved
Exclusively distributed by Hal Leonard MGB, a Hal Leonard Corporation company.

www.halleonard.com

TABLE OF CONTENTS

The price of this publication includes access to companion play-along recordings available online, for download or streaming, using the unique code found on the title page. Visit **www.halleonard.com/mylibrary** and enter the access code.

It's Fun to Play the Flute!

This book will guide you in learning how to play the flute. You will learn a lot about music and your instrument while playing both new and centuries old tunes from a variety of cultures.

Perhaps you've already learned another instrument, or have received elementary musical training. If so, you've got a head start that will serve you well. If not, this method requires no previous experience and will enable you, in easy steps, to learn your instrument while gaining knowledge of basic music theory. If there's something you don't understand, or need to know more about, you can ask your flute teacher.

The book begins with tone exercises using only the head joint. Take your time! Practicing on the head joint will give you a good feel for tone development before moving on to playing position and fingering issues. Fingerings will be introduced in easy steps with appropriate practice modules. Each will be followed by a tune that utilizes newly learned notes. Along the way, you'll learn about musical terminology, notes, rhythm, and famous composers.

Exercise — Exercises present material to help you master various techniques.

Tip — Tips warn about common mistakes, or offer review material from previous lessons.

Activity — Activities indicate exercises that encourage the use of imagination in arranging music, as well as other musical games and ideas.

It's especially fun to play the flute and make music with others. You'll find that most pieces in this book are written in two-part harmony so you can play together with your teacher or a fellow music student! The tunes will sound just as good when played together with other instruments, such as the violin, oboe, or recorder.

Online Audio

Songs featuring this symbol are recorded and are available for download or streaming. To access the companion recordings online, visit: www.halleonard.com/mylibrary and enter the code printed on the title page of this book. Here you can listen to each tune as recorded by the authors. If your listening device has a balance switch, you can fade out the top line in the music and play the first flute part alone with the accompaniment.

In the back of this book you'll find some exercises to do without your instrument. These will aid in the development of your breathing, and in the strengthening of your lips, tongue, and fingers. They are devised to compliment your normal practice routine.

Chapter 1
Getting Started: Playing on the Head Joint

The most important parts of the flute are the head joint and embouchure plate. This is where your sound originates. Try blowing into the head joint as indicated in the pictures below. Make sure the open end of the head joint is to your right. Did a sound come out? Great! If not don't worry, that's normal at first. Just keep trying!

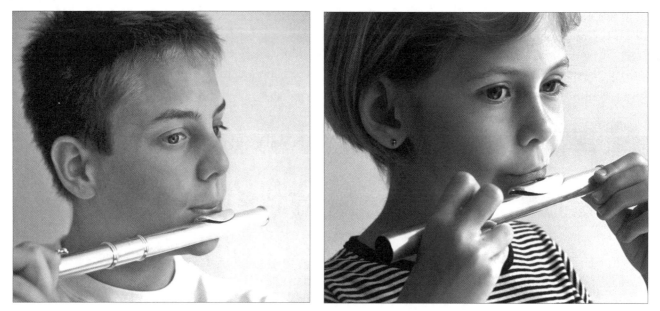

Everything you do with your mouth (especially the lips) to get sound is called your embouchure.

Here are some tips:

- Place your lower lip to the embouchure plate so that the lip covers about one third of the mouth hole.

- Spread your lips slightly while lightly tensing your lips and the corners of your mouth. Imagine you're spitting out a grape seed.

- Try some different lip positions when you blow:

    – smiling, grinning, saying "oohee," "yay," or "we"

    – slightly raising or lowering the corners of your mouth

    – moving the jaw with the lower lip back and forth

    – slightly rolling the head joint towards or away from you

- Check yourself in the mirror! Do you look like the students in the pictures above, or like your teacher?

- Repeat often every day. Your lip muscles need to get used to the embouchure formation.

- Spitting water (as pictured) can help you get a feel for the form and direction of your airstream:

    – Take a mouthful of water and blow it out in a thin stream with a high arc.

Tip   Proper breathing will aid in your tone production. The breathing exercises on page 60 will be a part of your daily flute practice from the beginning. They are intended to train your breathing muscles, especially the diaphragm and stomach muscles.

Lip training also aids in embouchure development, as described on page 62.

Tonguing

You should be getting a feel for embouchure and tone formation. Now let's try getting a clear start on our notes. Center the tip of your tongue to the back of your two top front teeth. Then use the syllable "doo" to start the note. To end the note, just stop the airstream.

Each group of notes begins with a clean, clear tongue attack, and each following note will be tongued separately in this manner.

Exercise

E1   Try playing tones and pauses of varying lengths:

dooooooooo   doo doo   doooooooooooo   doo   doooo doooo   doooooooooooo   doo

Activity   Create some music of your own using long tones of differing lengths. Write them down like in E1 and play them!

Exercise

E2   Try again using different words like your name or the names of your siblings and friends!

Mo-ni-ca   Stev-en   Gab-ri-el-a   Ben-ja-min

Activity   **Quiz for Family, Friends, and Teachers**

Play a song you know on the head joint for a family member, a friend, or your teacher. Can your listener guess which song it is just through the rhythms of your sounds?

Note Values

Most of the music you'll be playing will be written down in music notation (notated). The different note values identify how long the notes and rests will be held, as well as their sequence (**rhythm**):

Quarter Note ♩   Quarter Rest 𝄽

Equal divisions, or beats, are often grouped in quarters. The quarter note is one beat long.

The **half note** is twice as long ♩   so is the **half rest** ▬

The **whole note** is four times as long ○   so is the **whole rest** ▬

The **eighth note** is half as long ♪   so is the **eighth rest** ♪

Lots of eighth notes in a row are usually connected with a beam rather than a flag:

♪♪♪♪♪ = ♫ ♫ = ♬

Meter

Just as in the language we speak, there are differing accents in music. Beats and their varying accents are usually grouped into **measures** or **bars**, which are separated by **bar lines**. Thus, a 4/4 measure has four beats, a 3/4 measure has three, a 2/4 measure has two, etc.

As a general rule, the first beat in a measure is accented.

Exercise Speak and play through the following exercises. Tap your foot on each beat so you won't forget the rests.

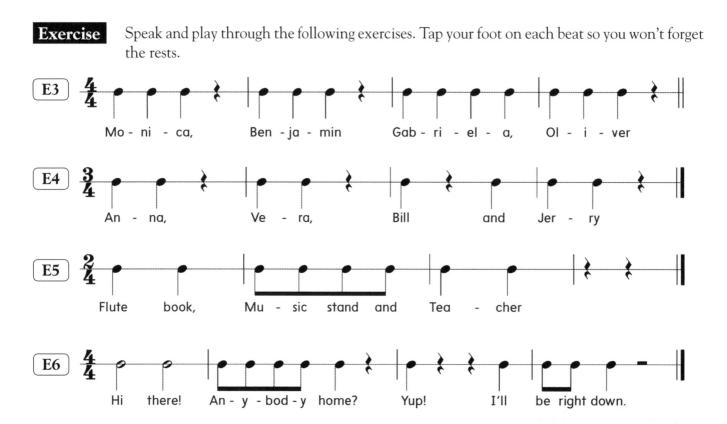

Pickup Many words begin with an unaccented syllable. Similarly, lots of songs begin with an unaccented pickup note (see exercises 7 and 11). The value of the pickup note is subtracted from the last measure of the piece.

Exercise

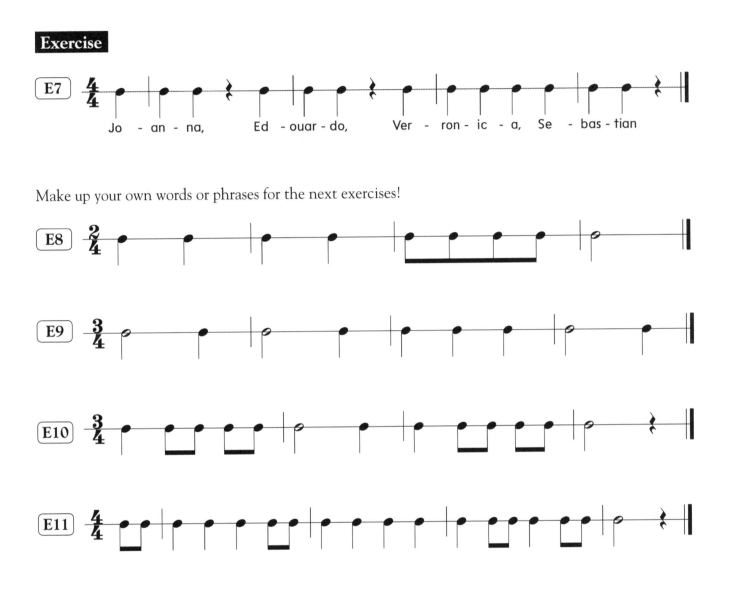

E7 Jo - an - na,   Ed - ouar - do,   Ver - ron - ic - a, Se - bas - tian

Make up your own words or phrases for the next exercises!

Activity Think up some more exercises like these. Write them out and play them on the lines provided:

Chapter 2
Blowing Speed

Cover the open end of the head joint with your hand. Blow and you will hear a low note. Blow harder and you will produce a higher note. The higher note is produced because of:

- a faster airstream (increased air pressure)
- a smaller hole between the lips
- a slight projection of the jaw and lower lip
- momentum and strength and support from the abdominal region
- the use of "doo" as the articulation vowel

Imagine you're plugging a garden hose or a faucet with your finger – you'll get a thinner spray that travels faster and further. Try this with your airstream!

Breathing exercises, lip gymnastics (pages 60-62), and the water-blowing exercise on page 4 will all help you to master the technique of how to blow harder and produce higher tones.

Legato | Covered Head Joint Exercises

Cover the open end of the head joint like in the photo. Play each two-note group detached (by saying "day" and " doo"), and then tied together (with " doo" and "ooo") without tonguing between. *This manner of playing where we "tie" the notes together is called legato.*

Rule

When an arc, called a slur, is written over a sequence of notes, the notes should be played legato (slurred) without tonguing in between. Only the first note in a slurred group should be tongued.

Exercise The "V" symbol indicates where to take a new breath between note groupings.

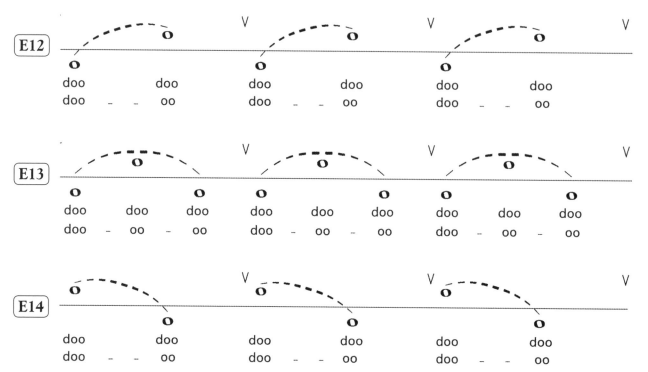

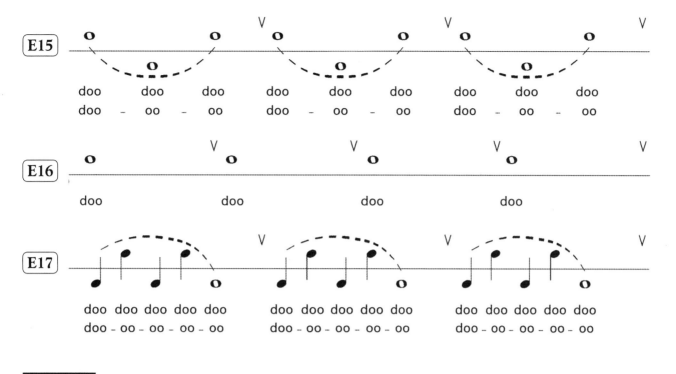

Exercise Play the following exercises and compose your own exercises using high and low tones! You can even add words and phrases to match the rhythm.

E20 Glissando (sliding up and down between low and high notes)

Play the little wavy lines pictured below. Use both a covered and open end head joint. Use more or less air to play in different octaves.

To play a glissando you will:

- alternate pushing forward, pulling back, and dropping the lower lip and jaw (ooh-aah-ooh-aah-ooh-aah)
- roll the head joint back and forth
- raise and lower your head

Practice each one of these techniques. You'll develop a flexible embouchure. Later, you'll employ the same techniques (especially the first one) for pitch adjustment.

You can also make a glissando by sticking a finger in the open end of the head joint.

Activity **Create Your Own Music!**

You can already make music with the few tones we've learned, either through spontaneous creation (improvisation) or by planning it out and writing it down (composition).

Try to depict feelings, emotions, or other themes musically. For example you could portray happiness, sadness, anger, wind, rain, something scary, an argument, a funny dance, etc.

Which musical qualities help you to describe each of the above?

Dynamics, speed, octave, note-length, rests, etc.?

CHAPTER 3
Now Let's Play with the Whole Flute!

Before you start, check out some of these helpful tips!

Assembling the Flute

Carefully connect the head joint, body joint, and foot joint through gentle twisting maneuvers. Be careful not to bend the sensitive key system. It is best to grasp each joint by its ends when connecting. Use the same care when disassembling or cleaning the parts.

Rule

When connecting the 3 joints you will, generally, create a straight line from the embouchure plate on the head joint, the large open tone holes on the middle joint, and the shaft of the foot joint.

Each flutist will find his or her own preferred position through small adjustments and trial and error. Your teacher will assist you. When you've found the optimal adjustment, mark each joint with a non-permanent marker to simplify the assembly process. Later on, when your playing position and embouchure stabilize, you can apply a permanent marking with small dots of nail polish.

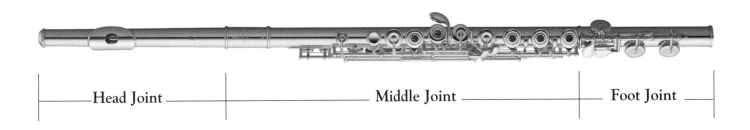

Head Joint   Middle Joint   Foot Joint

Tuning

To tune most common instruments, the head joint should not be fully inserted into the middle joint, but rather pulled out very slightly. When you play with other instruments (or with the play-along audio) that are tuned higher or lower, you'll need to adjust.

- You can tune higher by pushing in the head joint to shorten the instrument.
- You can tune lower by pulling out the head joint to lengthen the instrument.

Playing Posture

- Stand with both legs firm yet pliable, rooted on the floor. Don't lock the knees.

- Keep the upper body in an upright position. Extend pelvis a bit to stabilize the arch of the back if necessary.

- Angle head and upper body to the left to decrease right shoulder tension.

- Keep elbows lightly and loosely raised and the thorax "open."

- Keep shoulders loose.

- Hold head high.

- To promote proper breathing and viable playing posture, you should always play in a standing position, even when practicing.

Music Stands

Your music stand will be a great aid to maintaining proper playing posture.

- Adjust the stand so that your music is nearly at eye-level to assure upright posture.

- The stand should be placed at a 45-degree angle left of the feet, corresponding to a left-facing playing position.

The Hands

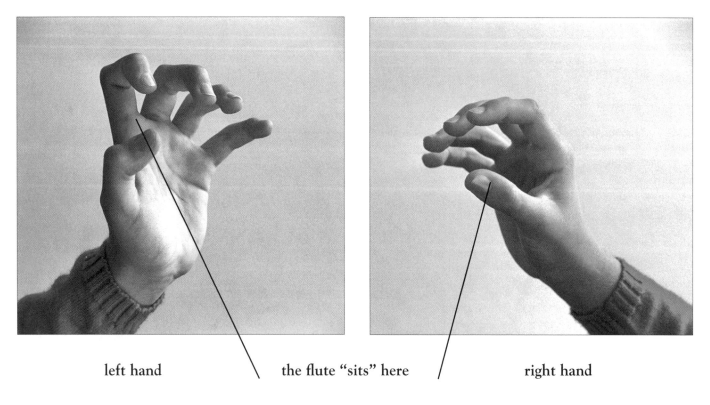

left hand   the flute "sits" here   right hand

The Fingers

Check that the fingers maintain an arched position. This promotes maximum mobility of the finger system, resulting in faster and more exact movement as opposed to a flat finger stretch. The fingertips should press in the middle of each key, not on the outer rim. Your right wrist should be held parallel to the flute. Avoid tilting inward. If you're learning on a flute with open holes you'll find that the construction of its key mechanism aids in maintaining proper finger position.

Tip Checkup:

Practice in front of the mirror! Is your posture correct? How is your finger position?

Fingering Diagram

Not all of the keys on the flute require your fingers to activate them. Those that don't are crossed out in the diagram below. When you're getting started, try attaching a piece of tape or an adhesive bandage to each of these keys. This way you'll notice immediately if you've hit the wrong one!

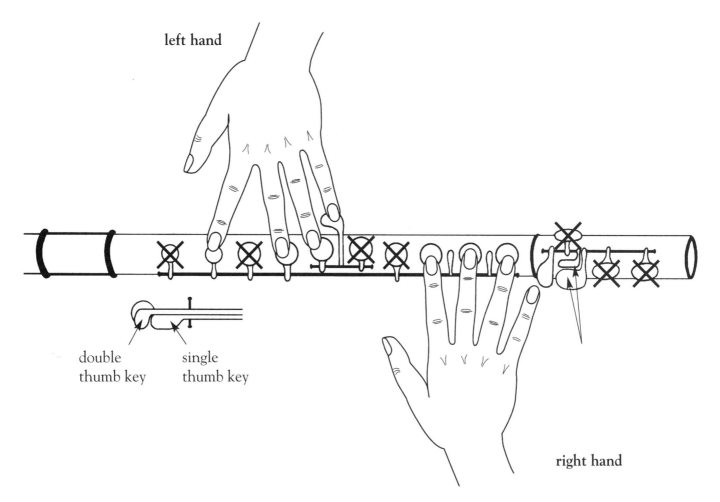

In the following diagrams, the "blind" keys are not shown. Here you'll see the keys portrayed as circles. A black circle indicates a key to be pressed. The G-sharp key for the left hand little finger appears in the diagram only when it's needed.

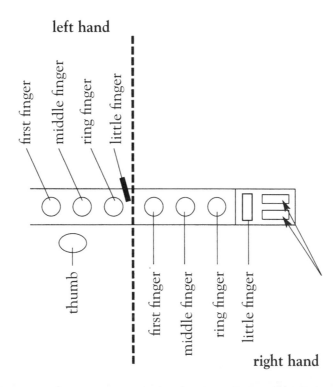

CHAPTER 4
First Notes: B, A, and G

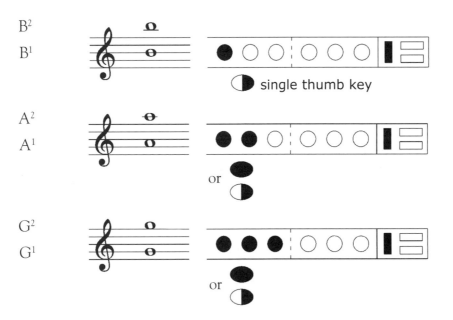

The placement of the printed note on or between the bar lines will indicate the pitch. The treble clef sign (which actually resembles a decorative G) encircles the line reserved for the pitch G1. The space above the G-line belongs to the pitch A1, and the next line above is pitch B1. If the five bar lines are not enough to accommodate all the remaining pitches, ledger lines are added either above or below the staff. Step by step, we'll get to know all the notes on your flute with their corresponding fingerings.

Tip To start, we'll always use the single thumb key, despite the fact that the notes A and G can also be produced with the double thumb key.

As you can see in the diagram at the beginning of this chapter, it's possible to play two notes using the same fingering: the basic note and, by blowing harder, the same note an octave higher. All the notes we'll be learning up until Chapter 10 can be played in two octaves without changing the fingering. Likewise, all the tunes we'll learn up until Chapter 10 were chosen so that you can play them a) in the lower register or b) in the higher register without changing fingerings. It makes sense to learn to play in both registers, even if one or the other is harder for you. If a particular register proves difficult, you can still play all the exercises and tunes through Chapter 10 using the register that "speaks" easiest. Later, review them using the more difficult register. You'll see that this manner of practicing makes the more challenging material easier the second time around. You and your teacher should decide which method of practice is best for you.

Exercise ## Tone Exercises

Hold these notes out as long as possible. Repeat often.

  This symbol appears above a selected note and means that the note will be held out for an indeterminate length. Usually it is held longer than the value of the note itself.

Octave Exercises

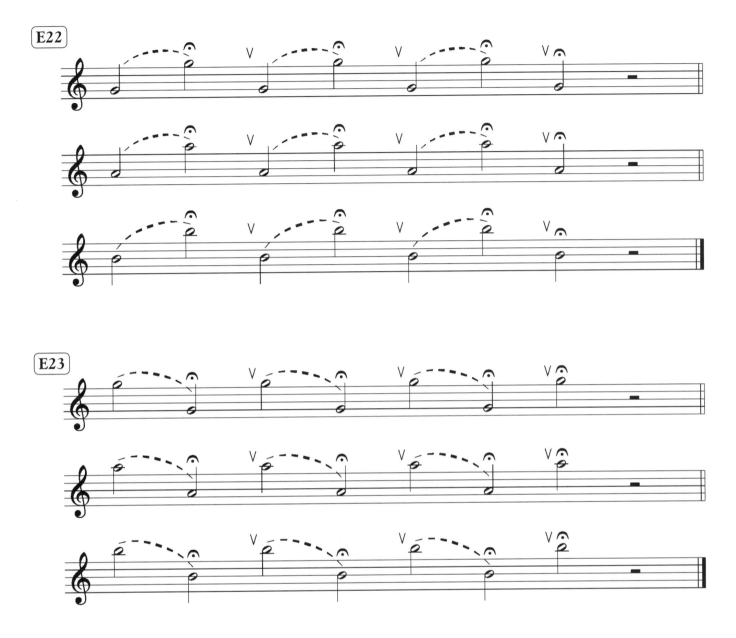

| **Tip** | Remember the hard blowing training you did on the head joint: |

- Place the lower lip and jaw slightly forward; make the hole between the lips smaller
- Blow faster air (not more air) streams through the smaller hole
- Supply strength and support from the abdominal region

Octave is a Latin word that means "the eighth" (step of the musical scale). Take for example E22. Starting with G1, climb the ladder of lines and spaces and you'll reach G2 after eight steps. Notes separated by one octave have the same name and are closely related: air oscillates exactly twice as fast at the higher octave (double frequency). Our ears are quite sensitive to this phenomenon. Listen closely! Are your octaves in tune with each other?

Interval This word stands for the distance between two notes. There are different intervals depending on how far a note is from another note. Intervals include the second, third, fourth, fifth, sixth, seventh, and octave.

Activity ## Ear Training

Your teacher (or a fellow student) will play some of the notes that you've learned on the flute. No peeking! Now try to repeat those notes yourself. Afterwards, change roles and you begin. You'll find that the more notes you've learned, the more difficult these games become. In any event, it's great ear training.

Variations:

- Play single notes only.
- Play rhythms with the single note.
- Play melody-like sequences of notes without a set rhythm.
- play melodies in rhythm.

1a. Moderato

Kaspar Kummer (1795–1870)

Moderato Lots of musical terms are Italian words, especially those written at the start of a tune that describe the piece's tempo and character. Moderato means "moderately."

2a. Lullaby

French Song
Arr.: E.W.

Kaspar Kummer *was a flutist in Coburg, Germany. He liked to be called Gaspard, as French culture was very popular in those days. His compositions for flute were highly praised, especially his flute trios which are performed to this day. He also wrote flute methods and exercises for his students.*

Activity A lullaby should certainly sound different than, for example, the following dance tune. How can you demonstrate the differences on the flute?

3a. Dance Tune

Irish Melody
Arr.: E.W.

3b.

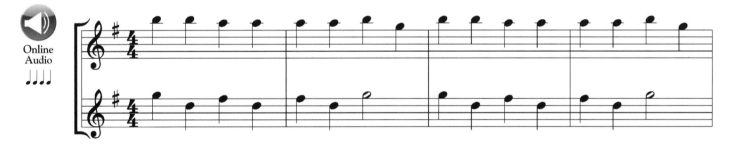

CHAPTER 5
New Note: F

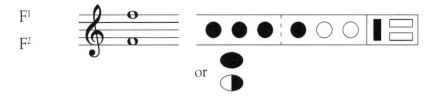

Exercise

Tone Exercises

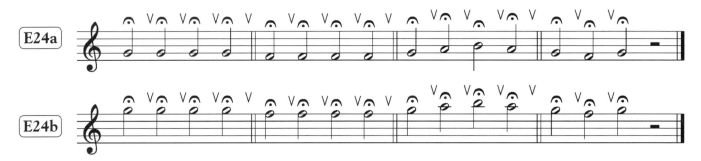

Octave Exercises

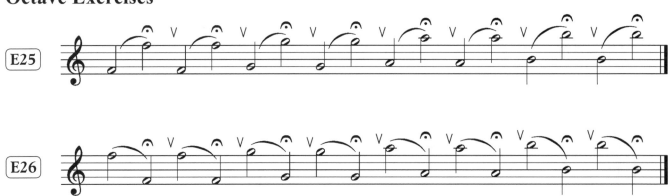

4a. Picking Cherries

French Song

4b.

5a. Rain Is Falling Down

English Song
Arr.: E.W.

Online
Audio

5b.

Online
Audio

6a. Merrily We Roll Along

English Song
Arr.: E.W.

Online
Audio

6b.

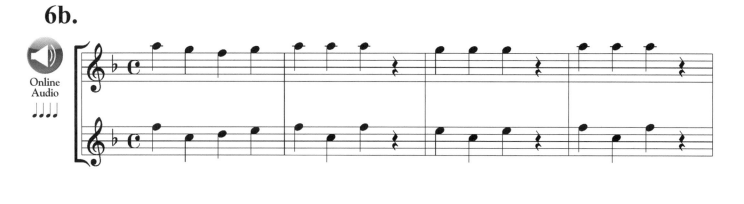

Online
Audio

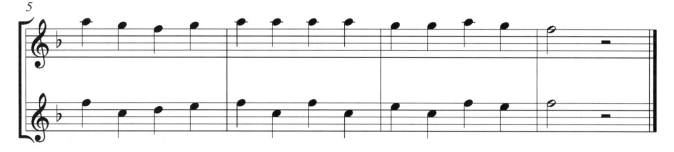

C is another way to write 4/4

CHAPTER 6
New Note: B♭/A♯ with the B-flat Thumb Key

Tone Exercises

Octave Exercises

Accidentals Accidental signs found at the beginning of the staff to the right of the clef form the **key signature**. This determines the key of the song. All notes that fall on a line or space with an accidental will either be raised or lowered a half step:

- A ♯ (Sharp) raises the pitch one half tone.
- A ♭ (Flat) lowers the pitch one half tone.

When you see an **accidental** somewhere within a piece of music (not at the beginning of the staff) it remains valid only through the measure it occupies. A **natural sign** (♮) in front of the given note will cancel the accidental or key signature for that note. This sign also remains valid only until the end of the measure.

We've already seen these accidentals in some of the songs we've learned. Up until now they were only placed after the clef sign and determined the key of the song. In the following songs, we'll encounter the ♭ (flat) accidental, which makes a B♭ out of a B.

Tip **RULE:** (for now)

If you see a ♭ (flat) sign on the beginning of the staff, play the whole piece using the double thumb key.

7a. Hungarian Folk Song

Arr.: E.W.

7b.

8a. Rigaudon

Henry Purcell (1659–1695)
Arr.: E.W

Henry Purcell *lived in London and was the leading English composer of his time. Two of his most famous works are the operas* Dido and Aeneas *and* The Fairy Queen, *which he composed as incidental music for Shakespeare's* A Midsummer Night's Dream.

8b.

Online Audio

Rigaudon is a fast dance piece that was popular in the Baroque era.

9a. A vi uma barata

Brazilian Song
Arr.: E.W.

Online Audio

9b.

Online Audio

Activity The **chord symbols** written over the melody lines indicate the harmonies that accompany the melody. Jazz musicians often read and play music based on chord symbols. If you know any guitar or piano players who can play on chord symbols, ask them to accompany you.

10a. We Have a New Governor
(from the Peasant Cantata BWV 212)

Johann Sebastian Bach (1685–1750)
Arr.: E.W.

Online Audio

10b.

Online Audio

𝄵 **Cut Time** (alla breve) is a time signature in which there are only two beats per measure, and the half note gets one beat instead of the quarter note. Although it can be interpreted as a 2/2 bar, for practicing you should continue counting 4/4.

♩· 𝅗𝅥· **Dotted Notes:** A dot next to a note lengthens that note by half of its value.

Activity Are you familiar with Johann Sebastian Bach's music? Check your music collection at home or look online. You will surely find some recordings of his works to listen to.

Johann Sebastian Bach *lived and worked as a hired composer in Mühlhausen, Weimar, and Köthen from 1723 until his final position as cantor at the Thomasschule (St. Thomas School) in Leipzig. Bach's mastery of the organ and his keen improvisational abilities were unsurpassed at the time. Bach composed a large number of important works including holy and secular cantatas, the Mass in B minor, BWV 232, the six Brandenburg Concertos, music for organ and cembalo, the Musical Offering, BWV 1079, and the Art of the Fugue, BWV 1080. His works for flute count among the most important in the repertoire. He wrote sonatas for flute and cembalo (or basso continuo), the Partita in A minor for solo flute, BWV 1013, trio sonatas, and the Orchestral Suite No. 2 in B minor, BWV 1067. His orchestral works, cantatas, and passions include wonderful flute solo lines as well.*

Chapter 7
New Note: E

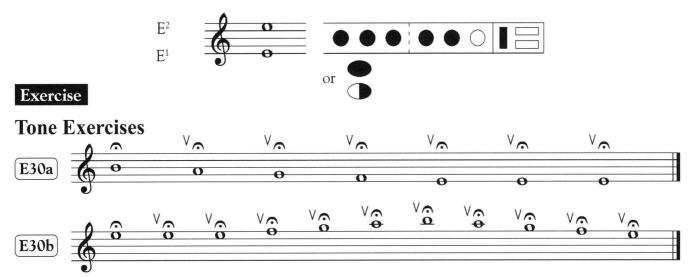

Exercise

Tone Exercises

E30a

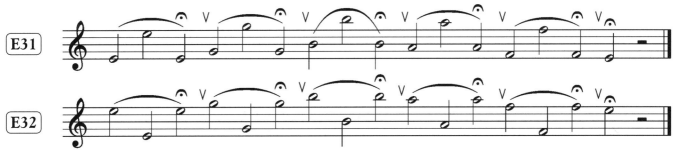

E30b

Octave Exercises

E31

E32

11a. Children's Song

North American Song

11b.

12a. The Three Duck Regiments

Lithuanian Song

12b.

13a. Hammer Ring!

North American Melody
Arr.: E.W.

Online
Audio

13b.

Online
Audio

Tip   In the preceding piece there are no flats (♭)in the **key signature** at the beginning of the song. However, in the second half, a flat appears which lowers a B to a B-flat. Since there are no B's in the song (only B-flats), we'll be using the double thumb key throughout.

On page 6 you learned about the **whole rest**, which is four beats long. This rest is not always four beats, however. Instead, it will fill a bar regardless of how many beats are in the measure (like in "Hammer ring!" with its 2/4 **time signature**).

Repeat Signs: The part of the song between these double lines with dots will be repeated.

    Play the song up until this symbol and repeat from the beginning.

These brackets are written over the **repeat signs** and indicate that we should play into the first ending the first time through. Then, on the repeat, jump to the second ending.

Tip   Sing this song first and you'll find the rhythm easier to master on your instrument.

Activity   You can have fun changing the rhythm or the melody of the song. Try it by substituting the following tones from the blues scale:

CHAPTER 8
New Note: F♯/G♭

F♯2-G♭2
F♯1-G♭1

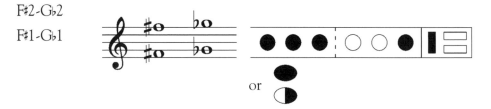

Exercise

Tone Exercises

E33a

E33b

Octave Exercises

E34

E35

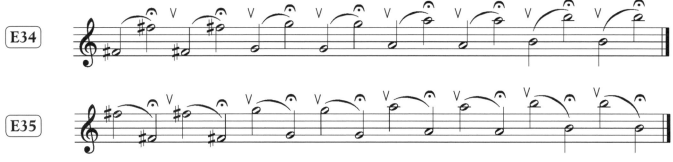

14a. Allegretto I

Bartolomeo Campagnoli (1751-1827)
Arr.: E.W.

Online Audio

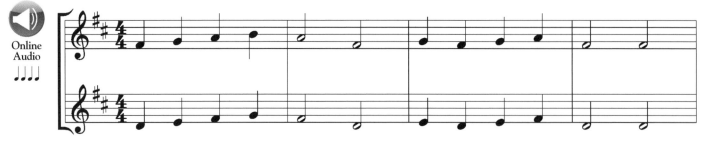

Bartolomeo Campagnoli, *the Italian violin virtuoso, toured extensively throughout Europe to high accolades. He also worked a few years as music director in Dresden and led the Gewandhaus Orchestra in Leipzig. Many of the instructional exercises he wrote for violin adapt well to flute.*

14b.

| Tip | Make a mental note: Because of the accidental in the key signature, the note F will be raised accordingly to F♯. If necessary, mark it in the part in pencil as a reminder.

By the way, it's handy to have a pencil around when you practice. Tie it onto your music stand with a string and you won't lose it.

| Allegro/Allegretto | Allegro means fast and bright in Italian. Every time you see -etto or -ino connected to the end of a word in Italian, it indicates the diminutive form. Allegretto means "fairly brisk." How can we play the song so that it sounds fairly brisk?

15a. The Month of May

16th Century Melody
Arr.: E.W.

15b.

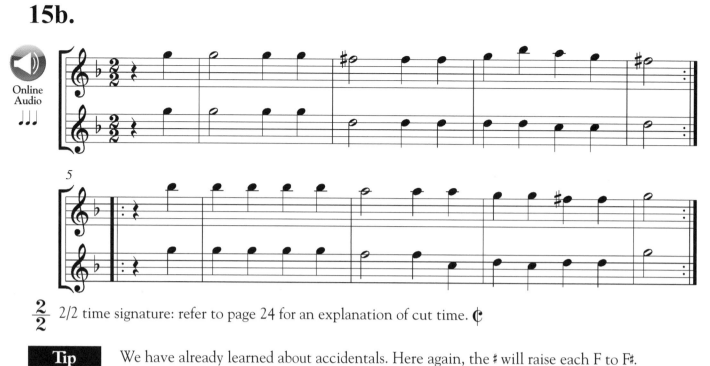

$\frac{2}{2}$ 2/2 time signature: refer to page 24 for an explanation of cut time. ¢

Tip We have already learned about accidentals. Here again, the ♯ will raise each F to F♯.

16a. Moderato

Kaspar Kummer (1795–1870)

16b.

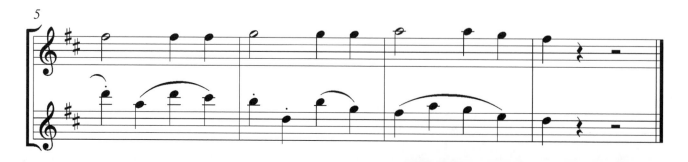

Exercise Connecting the note F♯ to E presents a special technical problem: the fingers of the right hand must move in opposite directions. The following technique exercises will help you coordinate the finger movements of such difficult transitions.

Finger Exercises

Check:

Tip

- Does your right little finger stay pressed down on the D♯ key throughout?
- Are you raising your right middle finger when you play F♯? Use only the 4th finger, also known as the ring finger, to play F♯.
- Pay attention to your right first finger! Don't place it on the key mechanism.
- Strive for a good **legato** while playing. Seamless ties that avoid unwanted accents, spaces, or sounds require very fast and precise finger movements and a consistent airstream.

17a. Mandandirun dirundán

Latin American Tune
Arr.: E.W.

Online Audio

17b.

18a. Tulu

Swedish Melody
Arr.: E.W.

18b.

CHAPTER 9
New Note: G♯/A♭

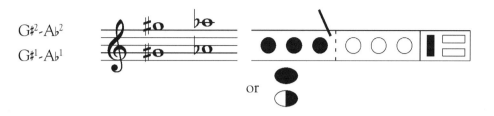

Exercise

Finger Exercises

19a. Taking a Walk

E.W.

19b.

Online
Audio

♩♩♩♩

Activity — "Taking a walk" can be played as a **rondo** as well (a song where the melody consistently returns with interludes in between repetitions). Play the theme several times and add interludes between these themes where you'll imitate some sights and sounds you might experience while taking a walk: the wind rustling in the trees, heavy traffic at an intersection, birds chirping, music on the car radio, etc.

20a. Plants on the Riverbanks

Russian Melody
Arr.: E.W.

Online
Audio

♩♩♩

20b.

Online
Audio

♩♩♩

Exercise

Finger Exercises

A♭ is a lowered A and is fingered the same as G♯ (raised G). It may be confusing when one fingering has different names and spellings, but it makes sense. In a musical context, the A♭ replaces the A (there will be no A's) and G♯ replaces the G (there will be no G's).

21a. I Caught a Mosquito Today

Hungarian Melody

21b.

22a. I Grew Like a Little Flower

Estonian Melody

22b.

We talked about the **natural sign** (♮) earlier. It serves to cancel any accidentals up through the next bar line. In this song the key signature calls for E♭, but when the natural sign appears, E♭ is raised to E again.

Exercise

Finger Exercises

Finger G♭ like F♯!

23a. Hungarian Tune

23b.

Tip

Don't worry about all those accidentals! Those marked notes aren't any harder to play than the unmarked ones. If you check which notes will be raised and lowered before playing each song, the accidental markings won't be so worrisome. Theobald Böhm (Boehm), the famous flutist and instrument maker from Munich, developed the flute we play today in 1847 as a chromatic instrument. That means that each of the twelve notes in the octave has its own key to finger, regulated through a refined system of key mechanisms.

Theobald Boehm (1794-1881) and his Italian colleague Antoine Sacchetti holding their Boehm Flutes. Boehm is portrayed sitting on the right.

24a. La belle Française, KV 353

W. A. Mozart (1756–1791)
Arr.: E.W.

Online
Audio

Composer and pianist **Wolfgang Amadeus Mozart** *created a sensation as he traveled throughout Europe's capitols before he had even turned ten. He produced an astounding amount of music during his lifetime, much of it now considered staples of Classical era repertoire along with works by Haydn and Beethoven. He wrote in all the major genres of the day, including symphonies, concertos, chamber music, and opera (can you name one?). He also wrote some important works for flute: two concertos, the Andante in C Major, K. 315, the Concerto for Flute, Harp, and Orchestra in C Major, K. 299, as well as four quartets for flute and string trio. During his lifetime, and since his death, quite a lot of Mozart's compositions were adapted for the flute. You're sure to find some of Mozart's works in your home music collection or online.*

24b.

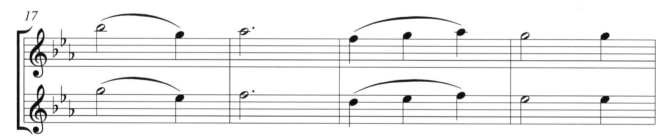

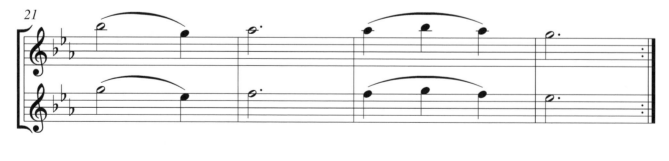

CHAPTER 10
New Note: C

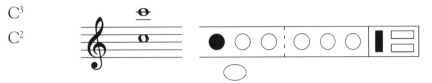

Exercise

Finger Exercises

Check:

| **Tip** | While fingering the C, you won't be able to stabilize the flute with your left thumb. It could be that your flute wobbles, your embouchure slips, or that you must anchor the chin more than usual. Make some adjustments to the head joint so that you can keep your balance. |

25a. Canario

Joachim van den Hove (c1570–unknown)
Arr.: E.W.

Online Audio

25b.

Online Audio

Joachim van den Hove *was a famous lutenist from Antwerp, Belgium. Like his German colleague Valentin Haussmann, van den Hove composed and collected dances and dance melodies, which you can think of as the pop music of 400 years ago.*

26a. Dance Tune

Valentin Haussmann (unknown–1614)
Arr.: E.W.

26b.

27a. Tempo di Minuetto

James Hook (1746–1827)

James Hook, *a contemporary of Mozart, was a composer and musician. He was well known during his lifetime, particularly among amateur musicians as he favored composing music that was both easy to play and true to the style of the day.*

27b.

Minuet The minuet was one of the most popular dance forms during the 17th and 18th centuries. It was originally a rather fast dance, but the tempo slowed down during the late 18th century. The dance's primary step is two measures long, which led musicians to determine that the minuet should be written in 6/8 rather than 3/4 time. As was the case with most Baroque dance forms, the minuet was first introduced to the French royal courts before becoming popular in other parts of Europe. This explains its various spellings: menuet (French), minuetto (Italian), minuet (English), or Menuett (German).

Activity Did you notice that a part of the minuet is repeated? You could change something the second time to keep it from becoming boring. Any ideas?

28a. Barcarole (from *The Tales of Hoffmann*)

Jacques Offenbach (1819–1890)
Arr.: E.W.

Jacques Offenbach *was born in Cologne, Germany. In 1833 he moved to Paris, where he wrote a number of popular works for the stage. He is credited with establishing the operetta as a genre carrying international significance. Many of his melodies became hits that remain popular today, for example the can-can from* Orpheus in the Underworld *or the barcarole from* The Tales of Hoffmann.

28b.

Online
Audio

$\frac{6}{8}$ A **barcarole** is a gondola song. The 6/8 meter perfectly portrays the rocking of the boat. The eighth notes determine the beat, so combine them in groups of three to achieve a two-part "rocking" feel.

Exercise

Finger Exercises

E44a

E44b

Activity If the holidays are approaching, you can jump to page 57 and play the holiday songs.

29a. Gavotte

Michael Praetorious (1571–1621)
Arr.: E.W.

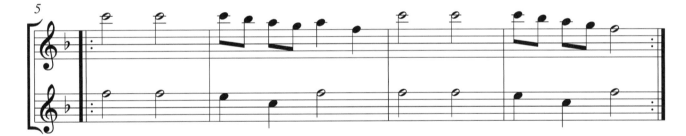

29b.

Gavotte A gavotte is a medium tempo dance from the Baroque era in France.

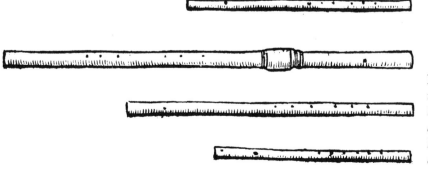

Michael Praetorious *was a famous organist in central Germany. He composed primarily liturgical works for organ and choir. He also wrote a three-volume thesis dealing with the music of his time, titled* Syntagma musicum, *in which he depicted contemporary flutes.*

30a. The Cuckoo and the Donkey

Arr.: E.W.

30b.

Activity This song is in F Major. Can you play it a half tone lower? Then it would be in E Major and the first note would be B. Try to write it down.

Transposing melodies into different keys is good training for the ear. It also provides good practice transposing different fingerings and tone colors into the new register.

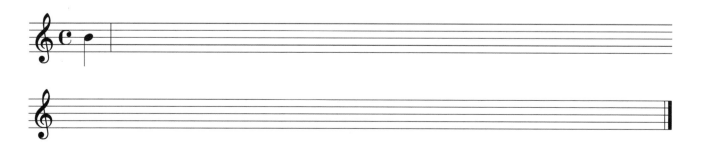

31a. Go Tell Aunt Rodie

American Folk Song
Arr.: Rachel Kelly

31b.

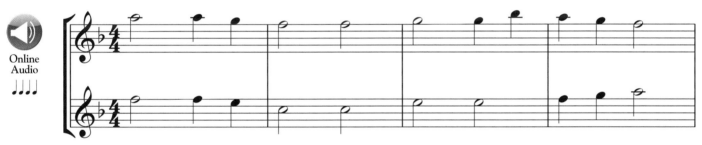

Activity You should play as much as possible from memory. Familiar melodies like this should already be in your ear, making them easier to learn.

Use all the notes you've learned to play songs you already know by heart, without writing them out!

- "Lightly Row" (start on C or B)
- "Hot Cross Buns" (start on C, B, or A)
- "Skip to My Lou" (start on A)
- "Ode to Joy" (start on high A)

32a. Largo
(third movement from Concerto grosso Op. 6, No. 1)

Arcangelo Corelli (1653–1713)
Arr.: E.W.

Online
Audio
♩♩♩

32b.

Online
Audio
♩♩♩

Largo means "rather slow" or "stately" – pertaining to tempo and articulation.

Articulation stands for the manner in which we shape a melody. With your flute, you have the ability to tie notes together (**legato**) or separate them. This separation can be shaped in different ways. For example, you could play each note short (**staccato**) or long (**portato, tenuto**), leaving rests in between each. Your choice of articulation can enhance the character of the piece.

*The Italian composer **Arcangelo Corelli** was considered the best violinist of his day. As a composer, he was responsible for the development of the **concerto grosso**, which served as an inspiration for later forms of instrumental concertos. Corelli's violin sonatas contributed to the development of sonata form as well.*

33a. Tune from *Don Giovanni* (after an arrangement from ca. 1820)

W.A. Mozart (1756–1791)
Arr.: E.W.

33b.

34a. Polly Wolly Doodle

American Tune
Arr.: E.W.

34b.

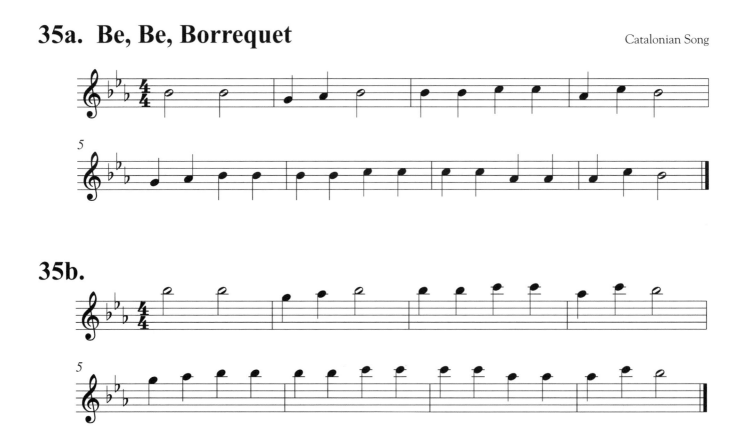

35a. Be, Be, Borrequet

Catalonian Song

35b.

36a. When the Saints Go Marching In

American Gospel Hymn
Arr.: E.W.

Online Audio

36b.

Online Audio

37a. Angelique

Haitian Melody
Arr.: E.W.

Online Audio

37b.

Online Audio

When two notes of the same pitch are tied with a slur mark, the second note is not tongued. The length of the note is the sum of the value of both notes.

Tip The rhythms in this song will be easier to play if you clap or speak the rhythms first, and also sing the song without your flute.

CHAPTER 11
Connecting the Registers

Up until now, you've played the songs either in the lower register or in the higher register. The next songs are different in that they'll combine both registers within a musical phrase. Before we play these songs, though, let's do some exercises to practice crossing register.

Exercise

Exercises for Register Crossover

Check:

Tip While moving from one register to the next you can maintain tone quality by adjusting:
- your lower lip and jaw
- your airspeed
- your abdominal support

Remember your first strong blowing exercises from page 8.

2 Canons

38. Let Us Begin

Fritz B. Metzger (1908–1985)

39. Row, Row, Row Your Boat

English Song

40. The Brave Cuckoos

François Couperin (1668–1733)
Arr.: E.W.

François Couperin, *known as "le Grand" (the great) came from a family of musicians. At age 30 he was hired as organist to the court of the French King Louis XIV, also known as the Sun King. A prolific composer of works for piano and organ, Couperin was also well known for his chamber music.*

41. Allegretto (from Symphony No. 7 in A Major)

Ludwig van Beethoven (1770–1827)

Arr.: E.W.

Online
Audio

Tip   Perhaps you've already noticed that it is difficult to play E2 clearly. Sometimes the lower octave joins in uninvited! There are acoustical reasons for this, so we must approach E2 with great care through proper embouchure and correct air support. It will help if you sing the note in your head or out loud before playing.

42. Dialogue

E.W.

Activity   First play the top line of this song. Then play the lower line. Finally, play both lines as if you were having a conversation with yourself. Make up some words for the song!

Ludwig van Beethoven *was one of the most important composers (along with Joseph Haydn and Wolfgang Amadeus Mozart) of the Classical style as it developed in Vienna. He composed nine symphonies, the opera* Fidelio, *five piano concertos, numerous piano and violin sonatas, string quartets, and much more. Unfortunately, he wrote very little for the flute, but he did write the Trio in G Major, woO 37, for piano, flute, and bassoon, Serenade in D Major, Op. 25, for flute, violin and viola, Allegro and Minuet in G Major, woO 26, for two flutes, as well as some arrangements of folk songs for piano and flute (Op. 105 and 107). A Sonata in B-flat Major for piano and flute exists in Beethoven's name, although someone else most likely composed it. His Bagatelle No. 25, "Für Elise," for piano, is one of the most well known works in the classical repertoire. You may well be familiar with it, but what about Beethoven's other works?*

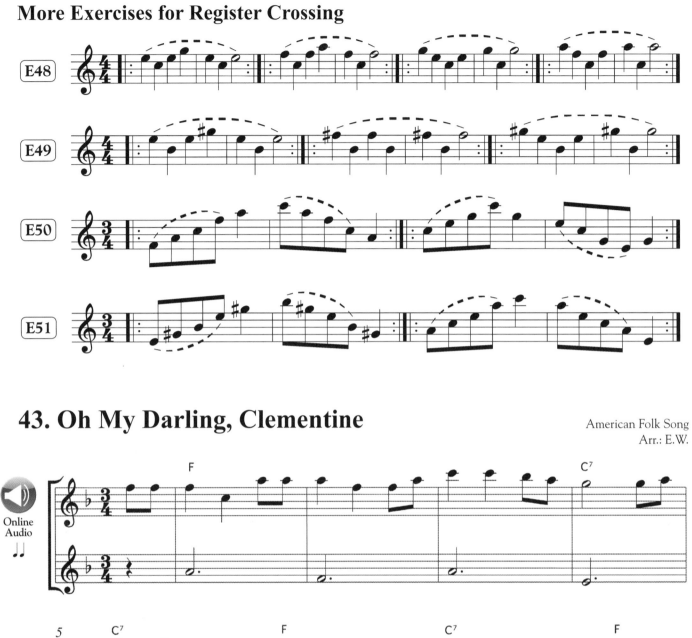

Activity

Can you play a couple more songs? Play by heart—without sheet music!

- Itsy Bitsy Spider (start on C2)
- The Wheels on the Bus (start on C2)
- Jingle Bells (start on A)

44. Melody from *Te Deum*

Marc-Antoine Charpentier (1635–1704)
Arr.: E.W.

45. Allegretto II

Bartolomeo Campagnoli (1751–1827)

 Here we see some notes with two beams, called **sixteenth notes**. They are twice as fast as eighth notes and four times faster than quarter notes. In the piece above, you can see how the eighth notes in the accompaniment line up with the sixteenth notes in the melody. You've already seen how eighth notes can be written with flags instead of beams. The same goes for the sixteenth notes, which can be written individually with a double flag.

This is a sixteenth note rest, with one more "hook" than the eighth note rest.

Rule: Each additional flag or beam reduces a note's value by 50%. Each additional hook reduces the length of a rest by 50%. For example, a note with three flags or beams is called a **thirty second note** and is twice as fast as a sixteenth note. The **thirty second note rest** has three hooks.

Activity How can you play this piece so that it sounds **Allegretto** (as opposed to Largo)? Think about which musical means you could employ to portray a certain emotion, character, or atmosphere. Recall the similar exercises you did with the head joint (page 9).

The French composer **Marc-Antoine Charpentier** *wrote operas, overtures, and predominantly religious music.*

46. Three Angels Sang

German 13th Century Melody

Online Audio

47. Joyful (Canon)

August Mühling (1786–1847)

48. Menuetto

Alessandro Scarlatti (1659–1725)
Arr.: E.W.

Online Audio

3/8 In 3/8 time the eighth note gets the beat, just like in 6/8 time. Each bar contains three beats. We can also combine the three beats into one, just emphasizing the first beat of each bar.

Tip Practice all new rhythms by speaking, singing, and clapping them. Here you see the straight eighth notes as they compare metrically with their dotted counterparts:

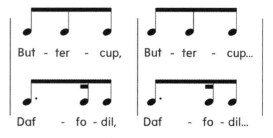

Alessandro Scarlatti *lived primarily in Naples and Rome. He composed over one hundred operas, 700 cantatas, as well as masses, orchestral works, pieces for organ, and chamber music. Many young composers were eager to study with Scarlatti, including George Frideric Handel and the flutist Johann Joachim Quantz. Scarlatti's son Domenico was also a composer, known for his many piano sonatas.*

Holiday Songs
Playable after Chapter 10

49a. Dreydl

Traditional Hanukah Song
Arr.: Rachel Kelly

Online
Audio

49b.

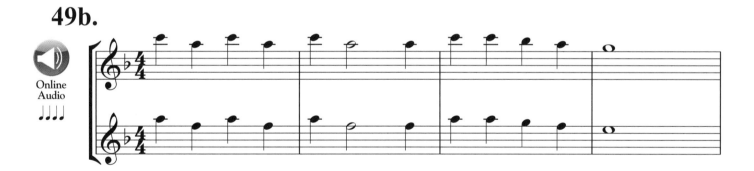

50a. German Christmas Carol

Arr.: E.W.

50b. German Christmas Carol

51a. Jingle Bells

American Christmas Song
Arr.: E.W.

Online
Audio

Online
Audio

51b.

Circuit Training: Exercises without the Flute

The following exercises strengthen the muscle groups we employ in our flute playing (and tend to forget to train otherwise) and serve as an optimal program for beginners. However, intermediate and advanced students will also profit from them!

Exercise

Breathing Exercises

Inhalation

BE1 Feel Good Exercise

Stretch your limbs as far as possible, allowing oxygen to stream into your lungs as you think about something very nice (sunshine, vacation, flute playing, etc.). Carry this feeling over to when you play your flute. Make sure the chest and rib cage stay open by keeping your arms slightly raised. This will promote proper posture.

BE2 Deep in the Stomach

While inhaling, let the air flow directly into your lower stomach. Fill yourself with air from the bottom up, and feel how you expand your middle as air seems to flow to your sides and back. Maintain your stance with loose knees, relaxed shoulders, and a straight backbone. It may help to imagine that something has just surprised you, or that you're smelling a bouquet of fragrant flowers. Of course we all know that air flows into the lungs and not into the stomach. But because we don't feel it in the lungs, we adapt to the feeling of pressure in the lower stomach while inhaling and call it stomach, or diaphragm, breathing.

BE3 Little Frog

Crouch on the floor like a little frog. Now take a deep breath in this position, noticing how your sides and back react to the breath.

Keeping the Breathing Muscles Limber (vowel exercises)

BE4 Strong Stomach Thrusts

p(h)oo-c(h)oo-t(h)oo-p(h)oo-c(h)oo-t(h)oo-p(h)oo-c(h)oo-p(h)oo....etc.

BE5 Gentle Airwaves

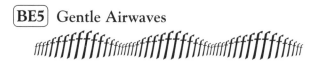

BE6 Shooing Chickens

shh shh shh shh shh shh shh shh shh ...etc.

BE7 Steam Engine (starts slowly and picks up speed)

shh   shh   shh   shh   shhh   shhh   shh shh shh shh
shhshhhshhshhshhshh....etc.

Strengthening the Breathing Muscles

BE8 Stomach Muscles

Lie flat on your back, positioning your legs so the spine extends straight, and place a few heavy books on your stomach. While inhaling, the books will rise with your stomach. While exhaling slowly (ffffff>), utilize your stomach muscles to keep the books raised. Always keep your spine flat and your shoulder/neck area relaxed. Repeat several times.

BE9 Cat Position

Get down on your hands and knees in a cat crouch, with your head hanging down. Have your teacher or a fellow flute student press on your sides with the flats of his or her hands. Extend your sides while inhaling to push against the hand pressure. While pushing against the resistance of the hands, slowly exhale (fffff>). Keep your shoulder/neck area relaxed and repeat several times.

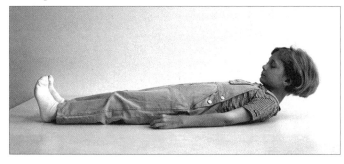

BE10 Head Raisers

Lay down flat on your back. While slowly exhaling (ffffff>), raise your head until your spine flattens and your sides feel the resistance of the floor. Keep your shoulders relaxed. Now lower your head while inhaling. Repeat this sequence several times.

BE11 Building Strength

Breath control is a major factor in flute playing and requires strength and support from the stomach muscles. Have your teacher, or a fellow student, press his or her hand on your stomach or on your sides as you play your flute. Feel the resistance as your muscles respond. You can try something similar by yourself: Wrap a bicycle inner tube around your waist and hook it to a door handle (see photo). While playing, lean forward to create resistance directly to your stomach or on your sides by shifting your weight.

Directing the Airstream
BE12 Blowing Bubbles

See how big a bubble you can blow using a soft, steady airstream.

BE13 Floating Ball

Lay down flat on your back, positioning your legs to assure that your spine is flush to the floor. Keep a ball made out of tissue paper or styrofoam afloat with your airstream (ffffff>).

BE14 Paper on the Wall

Take a thin piece of paper and try to hold it up on the wall using only your airstream (ffffff>).

Exercise

Lip Training

Enunciate the following syllables using exaggerated lip movements and grimaces:

LE1 foo-foo-foo-foo-foo etc.

LE2 oooeee-oooeee-oooeee-aayeee – oooeee-oooeee-oooeee-aayeee –etc.

LE3 ohyay-ohyay-ohyay-ohyay etc.

LE4 oo-ahh-oo-ahh-oo-ahh-oo-ahh etc.

Tongue Exercises

Pronounce the articulation syllables "day" or "doo" rapidly, using the following rhythm patterns. Keep tongue movements small and anchor your tongue by extending the tip to the back of your two front teeth.

Finger Fitness

Place your lower arms and hands on your desk with arched fingers, keeping them relaxed. Raise each finger individually, as high as possible, and hammer it back down while the rest of your fingers stay put. You can "work" each hand separately or combine both to practice coordinating parallel movement.

1=Thumb 2=Pointer Finger 3=Middle Finger 4=Ring Finger 5=Little Finger

FE1 Each finger separately: 1111 2222 3333 4444 5555 4444 3333 2222

FE2 Two fingers alternating: 12121212 3232323 3434343 5454545 34343434 32323232

FE3 Two fingers together: (12) (12) (12) (12) (23) (23) (23) (23) (34) (34) (34) (34) (45) (45) (45) (45)

Activity   Make up your own finger combinations!

FE4 Alternating your left and right little fingers, trace around a coin on your desk (clockwise then counter clockwise) or let the fingers jump back and forth over the coin.

What's next?

You've just completed the first big steps toward becoming a flutist! You've mastered the technique of blowing hard to connect the first and second registers and can already play lots of songs. Now you should review what you've learned by playing some of your favorites again. Chances are they'll sound better than they did a few weeks ago!

In the second book of *Let's Play Flute!*, you'll learn more notes and a number of new, fun songs. Recordings of the songs with strings, jazz band or piano accompaniment, or in duet with a second flute, are provided for you to listen to or play along. We wish you continued success and fun with your flute!

Flutists Elisabeth Weinzierl and Edmund Waechter both reside in Munich, Germany and are well known for their many concerts and workshops throughout Europe and the USA, as well as their recordings for radio and on CD. Their pedagogic work as flute teachers has led many students to become professional musicians and music teachers. Elisabeth is a professor of flute and flute methodology at the University of Music and Performing Arts in Munich (Hochschule für Musik und Theater München), and Edmund teaches flute and flute methodology at the Ludwig Maximilian University of Munich (Ludwig-Maximilians-Universität).

On the Recording:
Elisabeth Weinzierl (flute, harpsichord), Edmund Waechter (flute), Felix Gargerle (violin), Christiane Arnold (viola), Udo Hendrichs (cello), Eva Schieferstein (piano), Ladia Base (piano), Paul Tietze (electric bass), Werner Schmitt (drums, percussion)

Farao Studio, Munich
Sound Engineer: Robert F. Schneider

Musicians on Songs 31 and 49:
Emily M. Koi (flute)
Andrea Pelloquin (flute)

Tanner-Monagle, Inc., Milwaukee
Sound Engineer: Eric Probst

Alphabetical Song Index

Index of Musical Terms